SPRING
DISCOVERING THE SEASONS

Written by Louis Santrey

Photography by Francene Sabin

Troll Associates

Library of Congress Cataloging in Publication Data

Santrey, Louis.
    Spring.

    (Discovering the seasons)
    Summary: Text and photos portray the signs of spring—
buds, birds, weather, animal births—as nature throbs
with life.
    1. Spring—Juvenile literature.   2. Seasons—Juvenile
literature.   [1. Spring.   2. Seasons] I. Sabin,
Francene, ill.   II. Title.   III. Series: Santrey,
Louis. Discovering the seasons.
QB631.S257   1983   508   82-19381
ISBN 0-89375-909-0 (case)
ISBN 0-89375-910-4 (pbk.)

Cover photo by Colour Library International.

*For her special photo contributions, the publisher
wishes to thank Melody Norsgaard-Ashe, pages 8, 9
(top), 17, 26 (right).*

Printed in the United States of America

10   9   8   7   6   5   4   3

The harsh cold of winter is gone. Sunlight warms the earth, thawing ice-hardened soil. The air is rich with spring's sweet smell. Buds begin to swell on branches of trees that have been asleep for a long time. Birches and evergreens at the edge of the pond are mirrored in its glassy surface.

Each bud has a special beauty all its own. The silver pussy willow bud breaks out of its brown winter shell. It feels like the soft fur of a kitten. The sassafras tree has tiny golden blossoms that last for just a few days. The yellowish catkins of the birch tree sway with every passing breeze.

Last winter's snows have melted, swelling the brooks and streams of the forest. Clear and sparkling, the water tumbles and swirls over rocks and tree stumps. At the pond, fed by the flowing waters, the delicate leaves of the duckweed spread like a lacy mat across the calm surface.

The crocus is a true sign of spring. Its shoots push up through the soil even before winter ends. Now, as the days grow warm, its purple petals open to the sun. And with the season's first flowers come the bees. They sip the nectar, then fly off, carrying pollen to the next flower they will feed on.

Every day the sun rises a minute or two earlier in the morning, and sets a minute or two later in the afternoon. Around March 21 comes the first day of spring. On this day, there are an equal number of hours of light and darkness. As the days grow longer, masses of butter-yellow flowers—the star-shaped blossoms of the forsythia—gleam brightly in the sunshine.

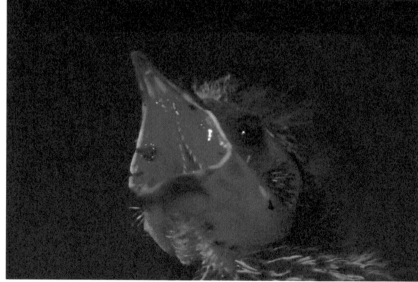

It is surely spring when the birds begin to build
nests and lay their eggs. In the low bushes or grass
of a swamp, red-winged blackbirds build a nest.
They make a nest out of twigs, grass, and mud.
After the eggs hatch, the mother and father catch
insects to feed the hungry, crying babies.

The blue jay perches high among the budding leaves of the white oak tree and shrieks its bold cry. This handsome bird has blue and white feathers and a small crown of bluish-gray on its head. The chickadee has a black cap on its head. It lives in holes in trees and sings its name, "chick-a-dee chick-a-dee."

After a winter of waiting beneath the ground, the winged maple seed opens and sends a thin root into the soil. Soon a twin-leafed shoot reaches for the sun. If it gets just the right amount of sun and rain, and no rabbit or deer eats it, this young seedling will one day be a tall, sturdy tree.

At the edge of the lake stands a handsome weeping willow. The long, slender branches, swinging in the spring wind, bend gracefully toward the ground. The willow, a fast-growing tree, is usually found near a river, pond, lake, or stream. It needs great amounts of water to grow.

The April skies turn dark and send down showers. Raindrops glow like pearls on forest leaves. The rain soaks the earth, and the water seeps into the soil, reaching even the tiniest and deepest roots. These thirsty roots drink in the water, then send nourishment up into trunks and branches.

One of spring's loveliest blooms is the wild violet.
The frail, five-petalled flower peeks out from under
its heart-shaped leaves. The snow-white lily of the
valley is wonderful to look at and smell. Its delicate,
bell-shaped flowers give off a sweet perfume.

In early spring a strange plant appears in the woods where the soil is wet. It has a reddish brown skin that is thick and smooth and spotted. This is the flower of the skunk cabbage. After a while it is replaced by broad, bright green leaves. Animals don't like the skunk cabbage. When a leaf is broken, it gives off a nasty smell—just like a real skunk!

Spring is a time of birth for the forest animals. A young fawn grazes in a sunny clearing, never straying too far from its mother. The mother deer guards her baby carefully. A fully grown male deer stands nearby. Last year's antlers have fallen off, and dark horn buds on his head show where new ones will grow.

Majestic Canada geese—with their black heads and necks, and white chin-straps—stop for a rest on their way north. They enjoy a warm afternoon of feeding and swimming at the pond before moving on. These large birds travel as a group to northern Canada, their breeding ground.

The geese will spend the summer months in Canadian marshes, where their young are born. The fuzzy, yellowish-brown babies are able to walk and swim soon after they hatch. It is not long until they follow their parents into the water. The mother bird cares for the babies, showing them how to find insects and water plants to eat.

The rare pink lady's-slipper hides deep in the forest. A kind of wild orchid, it has petals that look like a thick, red tongue. Another woodland bloom is the jack-in-the-pulpit, with its pretty striped hood of green and white.

Springtime dresses the trees of the apple orchard in lovely smelling pink flowers. When the blossoms fall, apples will begin to grow. Early settlers brought the first apples to North America. The seeds of those apples are the "founding fathers" of all the apple trees on our continent.

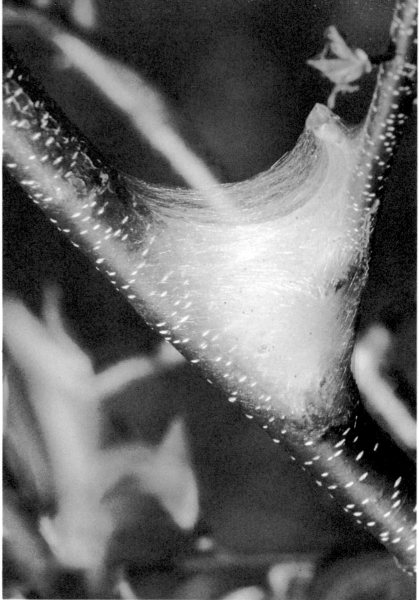

When the first leaves sprout on the trees, the eggs of the tent caterpillar hatch. These tiny caterpillars spin a large tent. Every day they leave this tent to eat the soft, fresh leaves on the tree where their tent has been spun. Every night they come back to their tent to rest. In a short time they grow large and fat, ready to leave the tent for good.

Two of North America's handsomest plants flower in the spring. The half-closed pink blossoms of the mountain laurel shrub open into waxy white parachutes. The four-petalled blooms of the flowering dogwood tree flutter gracefully at the tips of thin gray branches.

Spring is playtime for the frisky squirrel. The squirrel doesn't have to hunt for acorns as it did through the long, icy winter. Now food is everywhere—juicy buds on the branches of each tree, and soft, green blades of grass. When it isn't eating or playing, the squirrel is building a nest high in a tree.

The pond teems with life. A long-legged water strider, also called the pond skater, skips over the surface, feeding on tiny insects. Other pond animals eat the green, bubble-shaped algae. These one-celled plants grow in sticky clusters and have a bad odor.

Nature paints spring with a colorful brush, bringing a rainbow of flowers to the countryside. Fields of daffodils wave golden heads in the morning sunlight. Stately and satin-smooth, a line of tulips stands like a row of goblets on long, green stems.

The bearded iris grows in many colors. One of the most beautiful is the pale yellow kind, with its soft orange inner petals and fine orange veins. On each lower petal is a furry patch, which looks like a baby caterpillar inching out of its nest.

All winter long the chipmunk stayed hidden in its burrow. There, underground, it dozed and ate the nuts, acorns, and pine cones it stored away last fall and summer. Now, the chipmunk darts from its hole and hurries from place to place, searching for seeds and berries. Then back to the hole it scurries.

The shy cottontail rabbit lives in the cool, shady woods. It feeds on grass, leaves, twigs, and buds. When it is surprised by another animal, the cottontail sprints away in a zigzag run, or stays statue-still. Then its brown coat makes it hard to see against the branches and dry leaves of the forest.

Ferns are among the Earth's oldest plants. The first ones lived about 260 million years ago, and looked just like those growing today. In early spring, an insect crawls upon a young fern leaf, as it pushes through the ground. The leaf is covered with many fine hairs and is shaped like the handle of a violin. This is called the fiddlehead. Later, the fern grows tall and opens its feathery green arms.

Hundreds of kinds of caterpillars hatch in the spring. Each kind has a favorite food. Some eat fruit, some eat grain, and some eat leaves or twigs. Moths flutter about until they find the right place to lay their eggs. These eggs hatch into the caterpillars that do all the eating.

As spring moves toward summer, the days grow longer and longer. This is the time when the rhododendron shrub begins to bloom. First, the egg-shaped bud swells, until the purple-pink blossoms burst from their pale green coats.

Golden baby spiders spin silken threads soon after they are born. They wait for a good breeze to come and carry them away. When it does, they spin out a slim line and swing into the air like daring acrobats. The adult spider weaves a sticky web to trap small insects for food.

As bees sip the nectar of flowers in bloom, spring takes a final bow. The trees are in full leaf, the days are long and warm, birds sing through the night, and all of Nature is throbbing with life. The stage is set for summer!